LEE DUGGAN
VIA SETTEMBRE

Published in the United Kingdom in 2025
by The Knives Forks And Spoons Press,
51 Pipit Avenue,
Newton-le-Willows,
Merseyside,
WA12 9RG.

ISBN 978-1-916590-13-7

Copyright © Lee Duggan 2025.

The right of Lee Duggan to be identified as the author of this work has been asserted by them in accordance with the Copyrights, Designs and Patents Act of 1988. All rights reserved. No part of this publication may be reproduced, stored in a retrieval system, transmitted in any form or by any means, electronic, photocopying, recording or otherwise, without prior permission of the publisher.

Acknowledgments:

Sections of this this text have been published in *Noon, Junction Box 13, and Tentacular.*

VIA SETTEMBRE

Via Settembre

    charting available openings

        every

            spare

        gleaming

                potential

        half the page is empty

                picture this

    tasting Rome & transferring tickets

        my heart falls out

            of habit

        your mouth & now

            in my hand

            seeds storm through

                shutters

            shelter terracotta

            roof-top facade

cartography of imagined

        lemon geranium   hills

Lee Duggan

                                                            visible

                                                                        at a stretch

            strum in thyme

                               to

                                           reach

              speechless

                                                waves

     I hear but can't

               imagination

                                           too far for anyone

                                                            even

                                to

    pressed under

         paintings

                                              Via Settembre
                                              ───────────

                                    afloat
                                         drink back to

         lily tip
                cathedrals &
                              blue gods
            holding the line
 of sorts

                automatic doors &
                              embroider
                        when to get off

              granite sets against
     plane & poplar
            motors cold marble
                   somewhere new
                       plant lunar lit
                a crab head
                    flowing the link
              refer back
                    Lake Geneva over
                         Romantic flight
                              paint & lyrics a haunt

Lee Duggan

        each mouthful
   turn
     blue green flecks

         floor of earth
           angled in light
         the trees
           a brittle perspective

      turbines arrowheads & mathematics
    make shapes with our fingers
planning out of future
     narrow streets & little sense
       of change

ci sentiamo

        between waters
          stray to work

         stocking up
   tap in to
       unofficial regions

Via Settembre
―――――――

Gogledd

coastal

& dipping dramatically

    mules & fields of corn

      spread out all over me

downward Carneddau

    circled forest clearing

    translating home

pulled in to white

    cross skyline

below

a subtle blend

    softly urban familiar

read the moon

a systems theory

    changing the word

    to hear each swallow

din the sun

Lee Duggan

    dry twigs wake
        the quarry men   still
     stone fix from drift
      visible from the valley

              boned hillside
       broom
         dead wood
           & beetles
             set molten lines
          source sense
        Ogwen
           owls watch
          as you listen
              broken
      into dialect
           the heavens open
     strand line treasures
           mermaids purse & whelk cluster
          trained movements bend coastal
                to fix roads home
  converge into strangers
    stratam to stratospheric
   lost
    over & above

                                                            Via Settembre
                                                            _____

leaf sheath
            cultivar
         stem to stalk
                  too thin leeks
armed mattock pick

                              to

                                       the next
                                            best square
                  strim

                                   a patch of stoney land

chickens in a low sun
broken Italian
blood rise tide
& wine

hand me down

pass up today &
tomorrow take out sulphates
swallows & full moon
pull & you

Lee Duggan

    back down
        through connecting gods
to pass the day
      passage light
        solstice
            before the last
      swift

    the community centre
      eaves empty
        loudspeaker calling
    nests
      fade into background noise
magnetic gathering on
  high aerial
    move on
        forked & scythed
empty gestures
      to rich grazing
harnessing nature
        ritual acts & elements
      a spell to invoke the wind

        jik jik
      balestrucci skies

Via Settembre

       fall out of season
       & it's all available

soft C

St James

emblem of the pilgrim

gathering symbols

to cleanse the body

circle cast

& light candles

       repeat

     for effect

       recast

           open to possibilities

  finger shells

               far from shore

         cities & counties

     edge inwards

        fleshy Caravaggio

   Cortona & *conchiglie*

Lee Duggan

       incantata
back in
    ancient interpretations
                of age 16
    the world numbered from I to XXI
    in swords batons coins & cups
    excepting as ever The Fool
        traced to
              portraits & postcard
        treasures
stashed safe in a bottom drawer
 a silk scarf in a small box
                    still
    passed on
to a return
                kept
    before the gallery
           a life time later
mother tongue
    blazing mid evening
        suggestive to the naked eye
camera flashes & an overlay of language
    mermen ride
        the square

Via Settembre

        astronomical body

endowed with speech

                & loud-piping

                        Arion placed Orion

          waves crashing

                at the shoulders

                        setting sun

                confusing the celestial

     equator visible to every sky

            new city

          smaller & less populated

                    Poseidon from a watery domain

        in fury

     directed by landmarks

                Terra the Earth herself

       & mother of the sea

   lost to

      darker pigeons Trafalgar

to here &

      in every piazza

   pirated dolphins

Lee Duggan

        remnants of
      home
       lost to the familiar
     over written
with toothy grins
         expression
           all I take

        in the depths of it all
a blurred skyline
& no naming

today was under water
by all that should touch
the way the body sits

lack ability beyond intuition
                            seals mark me

       rewriting central to
        nothing spoken

Via Settembre

        a fresh watercourse

      where fish silver

from fry

         mercury formations

      broken at the skin

          & central to the season

    dull hues

      it gets dark

a coracle hung to rafters

     ash

  & willow

         wake me over winter

            more interesting options will arise

  early

      upper course

   everything

to

    seeing through

Lee Duggan

       low hanging

            branches

      beak first to dive clear
                   noticed
     by a small pair of river birds
          becomer of sand banks & boulders
  feet sweep reeds
       taste green pure mountain melt
    cold so I can not feel
              but never numb

   open to feathers & flesh
        bolt of trout
             out of myself
   watched
     & alive

           more than I am
  nothing else touches

              this dappled body of water

Via Settembre

    I become chapters of a botanical dream
            slender pre-spring stems
              wake you rambling
          folio of half sketched thoughts
              viscous material culminates under stream
        far from
          cumulous
      wonder

        copper-breasted
        directed by river
        a sharp down-pour
      pounding
      the windscreen

          strung algae hold
          thick the length of my hair
touched
touched
&
    felt
        zone of chlorophyllic shhhing
          arhoswch
& stay still

Lee Duggan

    is all

        channeled through
     a nod on my shoulder
a hand lightly
on some vulnerable
      curve
        small in my back
    sloped
        valley cloister

flushed through
        forests
    re-mov-re-mor cations
seeing Sirius everywhere textual
an intellectual avoidance
      rise to the swell & swoon
          repeating myself in
   galleries & pulpits

Via Settembre
_____

                in Holborn there are baobab trees

            Soames Square a wheel of life

        to close my eyes

        the birds open queries

you there now

                my hand safe in retrospect

take faith & the direct train

        wait underground

        slow slate flow

      not to look back

      or follow

the cosmos of wilderness

            pages of sunlight in gentle register

        rocks share lines

          strand trained movement

          hardly motion

        bending coastline ballads

                meet mountains & road goats

Lee Duggan

    whatever washes in
        the second hand
    misquote colours
        yelling like it could be

            out of moss & gate posts
            standing mountain shadow & stone

            ego forever in form
          I too have leave
            roaming desires

      draw an imaginary line
      dotted for continuity
    fields bent to lesser geometry
      curvature cut through
        & waterways

    as is usual
    marking marble veining
    traverse through land

Via Settembre

        concrete off-grey-construct
        rougher tones of the North
        chimneys remnant to industry
municipal areas clearly defined when seasons blur
networked motorways & delineated other roads
              plateau where the cloud flattens
                  to thread code formations
                  to navigate cultivation

    black white peaks
      colder colours
my body softens
      dark with wine
    first
    the shapes begin to turn
the future is with me
      reading Dante & fixed to the window

      land on the horizon
    a break with Europe
      think Irish/ Italian
    a weak link to Wales

Lee Duggan

        shaped by hedgerows & urbanisation
      subtle blend of pitch &
            pigmentation
   yielding the familiar
     to other
        dinned confusion
  clamour from bird call

         textures I can't fix
   in paint
      above & beyond
  pre-figure travel
       sky an abstract
       round time
    in & out perspective
   where nobody takes me
   & nothing is permanent
potential other colours
definition & direction

      shelter
    cliff edge warbling
       warmth in stories
     held close
   against every ridge

Via Settembre

    breathing the next
        regulate
  the way my mind
    against fallow field
      narrow streets
        & little sense of change

    walking cities
      I think trains

      keep within walls for local slices of whatever is hot
stray from work

    another clearing circled by habitation
stands out with Tuscan towns

      wind farms & the other type of cross
        white & regular

    forests broken into
      Palomino flight
    from Nokota to *stryd fawr Pesda*
  for better or worse

Lee Duggan

   when we were young
       we were in the middle of ourselves

        fact to quote friends
       written through my relationship status
 a history of being brutal haunting the work
          falling back on an inability to let go
         lacking value with make do
   next best never quite
       bite my lip & write inappropriate

beyond this clean house
deep dug beds
echo of a conch shell
calling brass corrugation
Hodgkins Green the cottage roof
cross rhythms field & country
art once a pulse
above the fire place

      which side of the island does the wind hit first

Via Settembre

        the bell blows over

           conductor of the pastoral belt

           accretion or gradational

      distorts through fared air

                & algae constellations

    on whistling sands

  cliff birds

          that tiniest orchid

          catch the light through three lenses

      pale sage blue lichen & mosses

              my favourite pastimes

              bigger mushrooms at Wylfa

        an alphabet of shells

        reference collections

in another

    metropolis

        closed roads & projects

plastic turf wound high waist bands

  boys become the traffic

Lee Duggan

      walk in barbers open all hours
mobilisation of dogs students & cycles
        accents signal free to roam

I could cartwheel right through the playground
      pop up bins a misspent governance

      funding family breakdown
      derelict shop fronts & open eaves

        under wing beat
    the dandelions are ragged
          spray below ridge shelf kelp
        high on wind rush
          hair faced half caught silent
   mallow
      bound to sit out
     & gesticulate

stylised splayed out patterns
missing beauty & catastrophe
formation roads run on

Via Settembre

terracotta connected by numbers & capitals
cut me through the alternative route
aerials replace chimneys as the world watches
on cruise control fixed to windows
    soften
        & disconnect
  the horizon

breath Italian
to forge links home
texture I can't paint
all perspectives
become my turn
      & take pictures
    take you
        out of this

    pre-figure the mark
      which draws

it's a contracting mess
8 lines in circumference

Lee Duggan

you'll have to refer to note books
all still green so far
won't see
        words but fragments

        nobody takes
                notice
        of internal rhythms
pounding temples
      alive

        pertinent towers round time
the whole way country roads
      sing intersections
    divide beautiful
      forms
          a perspective

    strips of design
        & intention
      suddenly architectural

Via Settembre

      set square borders of a sharp vista
    even the trees harden
        potential for patterns
            beyond me
        or new linguistic ambition
    to regulate this brittle star

      here through the foliage
  a mapped object
    barely a flash of blue
the trees at centre point

    collections of shells turn
to sand in my pockets

narrow streets & little sense of change
        walled towns catching trains transfigure home
      the way you hear
    changing the world
          as last late June
swoop sun din swallow
reappear *sogni d'oro*
      a constant thread in each other

Lee Duggan

        in grasp out of the rise
          a pastel haze made vivid &
            forever breaking
              see this
          to imagine what is tangible
           to re-imagine
            the fear of me in others
            met in convergence

an ancient gate to some imaginary footpath
        stranger definition
    blurs fairies & witchcraft
clothed in the sun with the moon at my heels
          I'm not from there
    lamenting fatherly relations
winding down to a crown of stars
              it's all boring in to me

swear ferociously my tower block babble
mix with it & try not to snarl
                    too hard

Via Settembre

      broken tongue

         full blood rise

       c softens

anon

        new material pleaser

    a down pour

forest valley

     & metro

   misquote what is left

      a bad taste forever on our tongues

      ways to settle the page

  where I fall out

quote the year

      when we touch

   we are in the midst of it all

  cross rhythm by heart

courgettes pumpkin & squash relate

shopping lists & shipping forecasts

  a bell somewhere

fardo in air

    cliff birds lichens & mosses all go in the *sugo*

Lee Duggan

    my own worst enemy
        shifting ideals
  unity & Sundays
          a found little map & options
which plot less complicated terrains
    times equating to cost
a flat media
coming out of pocket
to bird song & murals

        a loose connection
  prone to violence more than classics
closed roads & projects
      clean air
        ions in the wind
  time to stop

    back to a high fringe
    trees in pots
      al fresco

Via Settembre

    sly slide

    the opportunist

        glance sideways

           & all your friends are gone

23

        toddlers & teenagers

           design wheels

        second hand

          smoke & traffic

running commentary of the scene
annotation leaves nothing real
body beyond behind moonlight
systemic wood chop smell sap
my half decided a curtain pull
simultaneous govern liquids
stems & wiltage lingering in every voice

    listing dunnock

        the Irish man's nose

           coming through to take

yellow hammer chiff chaff

Lee Duggan

               held rock force
looking back to main land
                       glacial throughout

rock streak scrubble stream
episodic gaps nook front facing
hills to home upside crag
shearwater & guillemot
slits shadow skirt
wild rhubarb squirm
to unfurl fernish
flash mists
& recap

    scroll for older episodes
        a small boat & white wash
           planetarium of endings
    pull down earth
      puffin speck fat
burrow & dive

de-form the moon
tidal disruption

Via Settembre

      a charm of goldfinch
      trickling by the valley
        in loose Cymraeg
   eroding the particular
            stood where we are

   covered in ice

               set
                         50,000 feet
                      arc back
                          to take it all
          in
                    a fixated sea level
                        ships dip off
            dolomites

        lost purple

          cover

       earth science
   echinacea
      begin again here
      like code

Lee Duggan

        umbrellas
           set the beach
              features fly through

below land edges silently
to blues

                        how many miles
          can you see before the earth curves
                roads run river ways
                    cut by bridges
                  & turning back
        start within mountain range
              moving North
       clouds suspend into clear
                        still water

          making marble
      features
              topped & circled

      low lying mist

                    against

Via Settembre

      clearly defined

            crystalline

   atoms

     elementized

       to cobalt illuminate

              fixing the

                stark slate

    blue

  translations

    of home

culmination

    the valley below

no gods

   in the quarries

     wilderness

       of gently

    registers

repeating

      every phrase

      waiting for rhubarb

Lee Duggan

strong & reliable

beyond seasons & tears

      resisting my jokes

    compulsive nail brushing

      hanging on in my head

    like I'm on a permanent day off

        dress for holidays & gardening

feels further away

           this spot

    assuming the scene

body inside thought

        matter half drawn

decided exposure

    the moon governs fluids

      look back

  covered in ice

    planetary
awareness

    a unit
        of change

            currency
bashing rocks
  left with

        invertebrates
        & moss

www.ingramcontent.com/pod-product-compliance
Lightning Source LLC
Chambersburg PA
CBHW011309060426
42444CB00040B/3458